SELF-LOVE JOURNAL FOR WOMEN

SELF-LOVE

JOURNAL FOR WOMEN

Prompts and Practices
for Your Journey to
Self-Worth, Self-Care,
and Self-Acceptance

JORDAN BROWN, LPC

CALLISTO
PUBLISHING

Published by Callisto Publishing LLC C/O Sourcebooks LLC
P.O. Box 4410, Naperville, Illinois 60567-4410
(630) 961-3900
callistopublishing.com

Printed and bound in China
OGP 10 9 8 7 6 5 4 3

This Journal
Belongs To:

CONTENTS

INTRODUCTION

I AM SO GLAD YOU'RE HERE to start or continue your self-love journey.

Self-love fosters a long list of benefits, including improved mental health, increased motivation, and stronger relationships. Women especially can benefit from self-love to heal and prevent some of the stress, exhaustion, and burnout that frequently result from unrealistic societal expectations.

As women, we tend to carry a disproportionately heavy load that can include running a household, managing professional relationships, and keeping track of commitments to our family and community. Women also may be more likely to hold beliefs that we are selfish or should feel guilty for focusing on ourselves, and we tend to have a difficult time affording ourselves the same empathy we spend so much time offering others.

In the past, I felt like I was not good enough and used unhealthy coping skills to avoid and numb any insecurities I felt. But through my personal experience and years of clinical work as a licensed professional counselor specializing in helping women, I have seen how self-love not only improves the lives of those practicing it, but also strengthens their relationships. Since I started my self-love journey, I can now feel and sit with my feelings, manage negative self-talk, set boundaries, and accept myself fully. And this means I show up more authentically in my relationships and have more meaningful and fulfilling connections with others. My hope is that by experiencing this process through the self-reflection and tools in this journal, you will start to notice similar positive changes.

Writing this journal was a vulnerable experience for me, and working through it will likely be a vulnerable experience for you. We're in this together, and I'm proud of you for being here to grow and gain awareness and acceptance of the amazing person you are.

HOW TO USE THIS BOOK

Each section of this journal focuses on a specific aspect of self-love and includes prompts, practices, exercises, and affirmations. While this journal is designed to be worked through in order, you're welcome to jump around or return to previous sections when they feel relevant to you.

I encourage you to be consistent about using the journal but also to take it at your own pace. Self-love work requires growth. That can be uncomfortable and challenging at times, but it is important to try to have fun while doing it, too.

This journal is a companion to Rockridge Press's *Self-Love Workbook for Women* by Megan Logan. While the journal and workbook can be used together or one after the other, you do not need the workbook in order to benefit from this journal.

Self-love is a process, often a lifelong one; you may not notice significant changes right away. That's okay. Real change takes time. Continue to show up for yourself, such as in the ways you'll learn throughout this journal. I'm so excited and grateful to be on this journey with you.

SECTION 1
PROMPTS FOR STARTING WHERE YOU ARE

THIS SECTION OFFERS YOU an opportunity to reflect on your current relationship to self-love through prompts and to tune in to your mental, emotional, and physical health through practices and exercises. By the end of this section, you'll have gained greater awareness and acceptance of where you are, so you can appreciate your areas of self-love strength and know which could use some self-love growth.

My challenge to you is to respond honestly. I know it can be hard, but it's also hard to work toward real change without being honest with yourself. This journal is just for you, so be as open as you can.

"Self-love feels like looking yourself in the eye, taking a deep breath, and saying: 'I see you.'"

– ALEXANDRA ELLE

I am learning to focus on caring for myself as I care for others.

Describe your current ideas about self-love. What does it mean for you to show love to yourself? What thoughts and emotions come up for you when you hear the term "self-love," and why?

_____

_____

_____

_____

_____

_____

_____

_____

_____

_____

_____

_____

_____

SELF-LOVE CHECK-IN ASSESSMENT

Whether your perspective of self-love is positive or negative can have a great impact on how you move through your self-love journey. Circle an answer for each question to find out where you can have a more positive view of self-love:

1. **Self-love is selfish.**

STRONGLY AGREE / AGREE / DISAGREE / STRONGLY DISAGREE

2. **Self-love will help me accomplish the goals I want to achieve.**

STRONGLY AGREE / AGREE / DISAGREE / STRONGLY DISAGREE

3. **Practicing self-love means I care less about others.**

STRONGLY AGREE / AGREE / DISAGREE / STRONGLY DISAGREE

4. **I deserve to practice self-love.**

STRONGLY AGREE / AGREE / DISAGREE / STRONGLY DISAGREE

5. **I should feel guilty for putting myself first.**

STRONGLY AGREE / AGREE / DISAGREE / STRONGLY DISAGREE

6. **Self-love is necessary for my overall health.**

STRONGLY AGREE / AGREE / DISAGREE / STRONGLY DISAGREE

7. **Self-love doesn't add any real value to my life.**

STRONGLY AGREE / AGREE / DISAGREE / STRONGLY DISAGREE

8. **Self-love helps my relationships with others.**

STRONGLY AGREE / AGREE / DISAGREE / STRONGLY DISAGREE

If you selected "Strongly Agree" or "Agree" for statements 1, 3, 5, or 7 or "Disagree" or "Strongly Disagree" for statements 2, 4, 6, or 8 in the Self-Love Check-In Assessment, then you've identified some areas of growth for your self-love journey. Pick one and explore here why you hold this belief.

_____

_____

_____

_____

_____

_____

_____

_____

_____

_____

_____

SELF-LOVE MANTRA MEDITATION

This quick meditation can help you gently step into self-love by focusing on your breath, repeating a mantra, and attuning to your feelings.

1. Find a comfortable position in a quiet space to sit or lie down.

2. Close your eyes and focus on your breath.

3. Take a deep breath in and release it slowly.

4. Add a mantra:

   • As you breathe in, think, *I am worthy of loving myself.*

   • As you breathe out, think, *I am enough as I am.*

5. Pay attention to how you feel as you repeat this mantra for five breaths.

6. Take a final deep breath and slowly open your eyes.

What is your motivation to start (or continue) learning and practicing self-love? Describe the biggest influence on your decision (e.g., being in unhealthy relationships, feeling tired of negative self-talk).

_____

_____

_____

_____

_____

_____

_____

_____

_____

_____

_____

_____

_____

IDENTIFY YOUR FEARS

It's helpful to understand and accept where you are now so you can have realistic expectations for yourself moving forward. Check off each fear you currently feel to help identify those that drive your lack of confidence. Don't worry if you check off many, or even all of the fears.

☐ I fear others will judge me.

☐ I fear others won't like me.

☐ I fear others won't accept me.

☐ I fear I'm not good enough.

☐ I fear I will make a mistake.

☐ I fear I will embarrass myself.

☐ I fear I will be seen as "too much."

☐ I fear I'm a failure.

What is the biggest fear driving your self-doubt? When is the earliest time you remember feeling it? Describe the fear in detail to identify its roots. Write about the most recent time you experienced this fear. How has this fear changed for you over time?

_____

_____

_____

_____

_____

_____

_____

_____

_____

_____

_____

_____

CONQUER YOUR FEARS

By doing things that scare you, you gain confidence that you can do them, even through the fear.

Choose one thing you can do this week that scares you but feels manageable. Start with something small, such as:

- **Set a boundary**
- **Make a phone call**
- **Go somewhere by yourself**
- **Have a difficult conversation**

Once you've picked a fear you want to address, schedule a time to accomplish it, and hold yourself accountable. Consider sharing your plan with someone you trust to help you with accountability.

Joy is a positive emotion of inner peace that can exist even during difficult times. How do you bring joy into your life? Write about a time you experienced joy during the past month.

_____

_____

_____

_____

_____

_____

_____

_____

_____

_____

_____

_____

CREATE YOUR "JOY PLAYLIST"

Have you ever cried or gotten the chills while listening to a song? Music is powerful and a great tool to help you bring joy into your life, appreciate the present moment, and release dopamine in your brain. Show yourself love with more joyful moments. They have a positive effect on your mind and body, such as reducing stress and pain.

Create your "Joy Playlist," and take time to listen to it mindfully. Enhance your joy by listening to your playlist with someone.

NAME A SONG THAT:

Makes you smile

_____

Inspires you

_____

Sparks a joyful memory

_____

Makes you want to sing or dance

_____

CONNECT TO JOY

Children seem to experience the world with so much joy. Think back to when you felt joy as a child. It can be helpful to connect with joy by engaging in activities you enjoyed in your childhood.

Choose one of these examples or come up with your own:

- **Puzzles or games**
- **Arts and crafts**
- **Roller skating or ice skating**

Choose your joyful childhood activity, gather any materials needed, and schedule a time to do it during the next week. If you'd prefer not to choose an activity from childhood, choose one you have been wanting to try to inspire joy.

WHO ARE YOU?

In self-love work, we often talk about the importance of the way you think and feel about yourself. But the way you *talk* about yourself is important, too. It's hard to have a healthy relationship with yourself when you're not comfortable talking positively about yourself. Use the traits listed to help explore and define your identity in a positive way.

Circle the traits you would use to describe yourself:

Assertive	Kind
Authentic	Open-minded
Caring	Optimistic
Compassionate	Patient
Courageous	Respectful
Creative	Responsible
Empathetic	Spontaneous
Flexible	Thoughtful
Friendly	Trustworthy
Funny	

Taking care of yourself kindly and consistently is an important piece of self-love. How would you describe your areas of strength and of needed growth related to self-care? What is one way you could take better care of yourself today?

_____

_____

_____

_____

_____

_____

_____

_____

_____

_____

_____

SELF-CARE STRENGTHS

Part of self-love is taking care of your whole self, including your emotional, physical, spiritual, occupational, social, intellectual, environmental, and financial selves. For this exercise, you will focus on physical self-care.

Choose one color for each category: 5+ days per week, 2 to 4 days per week, and 0 to 1 day per week. Fill in each section of the heart with the associated color based on how often you engage in that activity.

I TAKE BREAKS TO REST MY MIND AND BODY.

I SLEEP FOR AT LEAST SEVEN TO EIGHT HOURS A DAY.

I MOVE MY BODY FOR AT LEAST 30 MINUTES A DAY.

I DRINK AT LEAST EIGHT GLASSES OF WATER A DAY.

I LIMIT MY INTAKE OF CAFFEINE AND ALCOHOL.

I MAINTAIN MY PERSONAL HYGIENE.

I EAT BALANCED MEALS.

■ 5+ DAYS PER WEEK
■ 2 TO 4 DAYS PER WEEK
■ 0 TO 1 DAY PER WEEK

List all the ways you care for other people.

_____

_____

_____

_____

_____

_____

What surprised you about what you wrote or about how much you wrote? How can you start to care for yourself in the same ways?

_____

_____

_____

_____

_____

_____

SELF-LOVE STRETCH

Women tend to report experiencing tension or soreness in their necks. This neck stretch helps release tension:

1. Bend your neck forward and slightly to your right.

2. Put your right hand on your head and gently pull your head to the right until you feel a light stretch along your neck (likely near the left side).

3. Hold this position for thirty seconds (or a length comfortable to you).

4. Bring your head back to center and repeat on the left.

5. Repeat one more time on each side.

6. As you feel the tension leaving your neck, imagine fear, self-doubt, and insecurities leaving with it.

7. If stretching your neck is unavailable to you, choose another body part.

Write about a time that self-love helped you get through a challenge and a different time when you did not use self-love during a challenge. How could self-love have helped you get through the second challenge?

_____

_____

_____

_____

_____

_____

_____

_____

_____

_____

_____

_____

YOU DESERVE YOUR OWN TIME

You made a great step in your self-love journey by purchasing this journal, so let's make sure you keep using it. Prioritizing yourself is a common struggle for women, and it can feel hard to block off time meant *just for you.* But committing to time for yourself is an important step.

1. Think about how often you would like to use this journal. How many days per week or per month would work for you?

2. Consider how long you can use it each time. Can you commit to five minutes, thirty minutes, an hour?

3. Block off these days and times on your schedule, so they don't get filled with other responsibilities.

I accept who I am today and believe I will continue to grow.

SECTION 2

PROMPTS FOR FINDING SELF-COMPASSION

SELF-COMPASSION INVOLVES practicing kindness and respect toward yourself during the highs and lows of life, and it's a vital component of healthy self-love. This section will offer you ways to treat yourself with kindness and respect, work through difficult emotions, and become more vulnerable by acknowledging your past trauma, which helps open the door to healing from it. Finding self-compassion is critical because it helps you nurture a loving view of yourself, improve your self-talk, and treat yourself like you would your best friend. Embodying self-compassion has been life-changing for me and many of my clients, and I hope it will be for you, too.

"Self-compassion provides an island of calm, a refuge from the stormy seas of endless positive and negative self-judgment, so that we can finally stop asking, 'Am I as good as they are? Am I good enough?'"

– KRISTIN NEFF

Start building awareness by reflecting here on your areas of strength and growth related to self-compassion.

_____

_____

_____

_____

_____

_____

_____

_____

_____

_____

_____

_____

_____

_____

SELF-COMPASSION MYTHS QUIZ

If you have some resistance around practicing self-compassion, you're not alone. Maybe you grew up believing tough love is the best way to motivate yourself or that being kind to yourself means you'll be less productive. Gaining awareness of negative beliefs you may have about self-compassion will help you shift them and practice self-love more effectively.

For each statement, circle the response that feels most accurate for you.

SELF-COMPASSION:

1. Is self-pity.

STRONGLY AGREE / AGREE / DISAGREE / STRONGLY DISAGREE

2. Is a helpful motivator.

STRONGLY AGREE / AGREE / DISAGREE / STRONGLY DISAGREE

3. Is selfish.

STRONGLY AGREE / AGREE / DISAGREE / STRONGLY DISAGREE

4. Helps you face difficult emotions.

STRONGLY AGREE / AGREE / DISAGREE / STRONGLY DISAGREE

5. Is self-indulgent.

STRONGLY AGREE / AGREE / DISAGREE / STRONGLY DISAGREE

6. Is making excuses.

STRONGLY AGREE / AGREE / DISAGREE / STRONGLY DISAGREE

7. Increases resilience and overall well-being.

STRONGLY AGREE / AGREE / DISAGREE / STRONGLY DISAGREE

If you responded with "Strongly Disagree" or "Disagree" to statements 2, 4, or 7, or "Agree" or "Strongly Agree" to statements 1, 3, 5, or 6, you hold some negative beliefs around self-compassion. I encourage you to stay open-minded as you complete this section, and I hope you'll feel differently by the end.

I deserve to show myself love, kindness, and respect.

Write about one memory of a loved one treating you with compassion and respect. Describe how you felt being treated that way.

_____

_____

_____

_____

_____

_____

_____

_____

_____

_____

_____

_____

NO JUDGMENT ZONE

Kristin Neff, a self-compassion expert, states that the three main ingredients of self-compassion are mindfulness, common humanity (which normalizes suffering as part of being human), and self-kindness. Self-compassion is not about making yourself feel better, but rather about acknowledging what you're feeling and holding space for your pain in times of suffering by not avoiding or ignoring difficult emotions.

Use mindfulness to acknowledge your emotions. Try it when you're experiencing an emotion that feels tolerable:

1. Turn your attention to your current emotion. Notice where you feel it in your body.

2. Label it without judgment (e.g., *I feel X*).

3. Sit with the emotion and allow yourself to feel it. Accept it, and try not to push it away.

4. Remember that the feeling will pass.

Self-compassion can help you build resilience and tolerance for difficult emotions and situations. Think about a recent time when you experienced a stressful situation. What did you think or say to yourself? How could you have applied the self-kindness component of self-compassion to this situation?

_____

_____

_____

_____

_____

_____

_____

_____

_____

_____

_____

_____

LET GO OF "SHOULDS"

I should be more productive. I shouldn't feel this way. Do those thoughts sound familiar? When you stop feeling pressured or shamed by "should" thoughts, you can release feelings of self-criticism and start living in a more present and authentic way.

For this exercise, keep track of the "should" and "shouldn't" thoughts you have this week, and reflect on the following questions for each one:

Why do I feel like I should / shouldn't?

Who says I should / shouldn't?

SHOULDS/SHOULDN'TS	REFLECTIONS

Self-compassion is powerful and can even overcome shame. Reflect on a time when you felt shame (start with something small) and rewrite your story of that experience through a lens of self-compassion. Apply the self-compassion components of mindfulness and common humanity to your story.

_____

_____

_____

_____

_____

_____

_____

_____

_____

_____

_____

_____

RELEASE STORED ANGER

Many women are taught that showing anger is inappropriate, and as a result they don't learn how to cope with or express anger in healthy ways. Repressed anger can get stored in the body and cause muscle tension.

Use the following progressive muscle relaxation to target your tension physically and release it. Skip any parts that feel painful:

1. Find a comfortable position to sit or lie down in. Close your eyes.

2. Breathe deeply throughout this exercise.

3. Bring attention to your feet, and tense all the muscles in them. Hold for five seconds and release the tension.

4. Slowly move up to tense the muscles in your calves, hold for five seconds, and release.

5. Repeat for each muscle in your body, moving up until you end with the muscles in your face.

6. Imagine a wave of relaxation moving through your body as you continue to breathe deeply for another one to two minutes.

7. Gently open your eyes.

Think of a difficult emotion you experienced recently and imagine a friend telling you that they felt that way. Write out statements you would use to support them, and notice how you can use these statements to support yourself, too.

_____

_____

_____

_____

_____

_____

_____

_____

_____

_____

_____

_____

GET TO KNOW YOUR INNER CRITIC

Jay Earley, PhD, and Bonnie Weiss, LCSW, identified seven types of inner critic. Knowing the different types can help you gain awareness of your own self-critical thoughts and recognize where you can use self-compassion to shift from self-criticism to self-kindness.

On this page are descriptions of the seven types of inner critic. Find the matching examples for each of these on the next page, then write down the corresponding letters on the blank lines below.

7 TYPES OF INNER CRITIC

1. **Conformist** _____
   Tries to fit into standards set by family, community, or culture

2. **Taskmaster** _____
   Pushes you to keep going and fears you'll be labeled "lazy" or a "failure" if you stop

3. **Guilt-tripper** _____
   Criticizes you and won't forgive you for past wrongdoings

4. **Underminer** _____
   Undermines your self-confidence and abilities by stopping you from taking risks

5. **Perfectionist** _____
   Sets high, usually unattainable, standards for you

6. **Destroyer** _____
   Attacks your self-worth and says you're flawed

7. **Inner controller** _____
   Tries to control your impulses around things such as eating, drinking, and spending

EXAMPLES

A. I have to read this text message repeatedly to ensure it's perfect before I send it.

B. I can't make friends because I'm weird and no one likes me.

C. This sweater makes me feel comfortable but it's out of fashion, so I have to buy something new for my interview.

D. I'm not good enough to get that promotion, so I'm not even going to apply.

E. I can't believe I called my new neighbor by the wrong name. What's wrong with me? I'm so embarrassed.

F. I love these shoes, but I shouldn't buy them, even though I have enough money.

G. I'm so tired, but I'll feel like I didn't get anything accomplished today if I don't finish everything on my to-do list.

Answer key: 1c, 2g, 3e, 4d, 5a, 6b, 7f

TURN YOUR INNER CRITIC INTO YOUR INNER COACH

Reframing is one of my favorite tools for self-talk because it allows you to see yourself differently. This exercise will help you practice reframing negative self-talk to strengthen your self-compassion by creating mental and emotional distance between you and your inner critic:

1. Give your inner critic a name to create separation. You might try something funny, such as "Crabby Cathy."

2. Use the left rectangle to draw what your inner critic looks like. Use the right rectangle to draw what you look like as your inner coach.

3. When you have finished drawing, use the blank fields on the opposite page the write four self-critical thoughts your inner critic says. Then, practice reframing each self-critical thought with a self-compassionate thought from your inner coach.

Inner Critic's Name: _____

INNER CRITIC	INNER COACH

INNER CRITIC SAYS   **INNER COACH SAYS**

THE COST OF PROTECTION

It might be hard to believe, but your inner critic is actually trying to protect you. Acknowledging how it's trying to do that can help you bring compassion to that part of yourself and grow your awareness of how that protection might be holding you back. Use this helpful practice when you're having a hard time reframing or finding compassion for your inner critic:

1. On a piece of paper, write about how your inner critic is trying to protect you, and thank it for trying.

2. Write down what your inner critic is costing you.

   Example: Your inner critic says, *I can't go to the party, no one there is going to like me*, to protect you from rejection, but it's costing you the chance to get to know people who might like you.

3. Take a few moments to reflect on your responses. Then rip up the paper to release what's holding you back.

Describe one thing that helps you feel loved and supported. Is it a person, certain words, an action? How can you apply this knowledge to your life during stressful times?

_____

_____

_____

_____

_____

_____

_____

_____

_____

_____

_____

_____

_____

_____

_____

_____

VALIDATING YOUR INNER CHILD

When you struggle with self-love, you may find yourself looking to others for validation. But it's not helpful to rely heavily, or solely, on external validation. This exercise will help you practice self-validation by showing your inner child needed love and support.

As you fill in the table, think about difficult (but tolerable) experiences you had as a child when you needed to feel seen, heard, and loved.

CHILDHOOD EXPERIENCE	SELF-VALIDATION
I failed a test in 8th grade.	I'm still learning. It's okay to fail. That's how we grow.
My first partner broke up with me.	This is a really hard experience. It makes sense to feel bad.

Choose an experience you shared in the previous exercise. Write a letter to your younger self. Offer more of the support, love, and validation that you needed at that time and that are still needed today.

_____

_____

_____

_____

_____

_____

_____

_____

_____

_____

_____

_____

_____

CREATE A SAFE SPACE

Everyone needs to feel safe; safety is an important part of healing from past hurts. Self-soothing activities can create a sense of safety within yourself in a loving and compassionate way.

From the following list, choose a new activity to practice each day this week:

- **Picture things you're looking forward to.**

- **Remember the words to a calming song or poem.**

- **Give yourself a hug, or massage your own hands, shoulders, or feet.**

- **Imagine a safe, soothing place, such as the beach or a loved one's home.**

- **List your favorite movies, books, foods, etc.**

- **Visualize your favorite place or the face of someone you love (pets included).**

- **Repeat a self-compassionate phrase, such as, *This is really hard, and I'll get through it.***

Describe what your life would look like and how you would feel without self-judgment or self-criticism. How can you bring more self-compassion into your life and use self-talk to be kinder to yourself?

_____

_____

_____

_____

_____

_____

_____

_____

_____

_____

_____

_____

SELF-ACCEPTANCE MEDITATION

Accepting your whole self will help you worry less about what others think about you. This meditation, adapted from the work of Louise Hay, will guide you to work toward self-acceptance.

1. Find a comfortable position to sit or stand in, in front of a mirror. Close your eyes.

2. Imagine yourself as a young child. Picture yourself in your mind. Show your child self kindness and accept yourself as a child into your heart. Take a deep breath.

3. Imagine yourself as an older child. Repeat the practice from step 2.

4. Imagine yourself as a teen or young adult. Repeat the practice from step 2.

5. Bring yourself back to the present moment. Gently open your eyes.

6. As you look into your eyes, repeat the same process to accept your current self into your heart.

Every part of me deserves my love and kindness.

PROMPTS FOR RELEASING SELF-DOUBT

YOU MAY FIND YOURSELF getting in your own way when it comes to reaching your goals. Maybe you hold on to mistakes, insecurities, self-limiting beliefs, and negative self-talk. In this section, you'll get out of your own way by acknowledging and releasing the past and working through deep-rooted beliefs about your worth and abilities. You'll start separating how others view you from how you view yourself, strengthening your confidence and sense of identity. Releasing self-doubt requires having empathy for yourself and your challenges, and discovering what will make you stronger. Are you ready to release self-doubt and get out of your own way?

"The only thing that was ever wrong with me was my belief that there was something wrong with me."

—GLENNON DOYLE

When did you first begin to doubt yourself and become concerned about not being good enough? Write about one example of how self-doubt affects your life today.

_____

_____

_____

_____

_____

_____

_____

_____

_____

_____

_____

_____

_____

_____

SELF-LIMITING BELIEFS QUIZ

Everyone has believed they weren't good enough at some point in their lives. The beliefs you hold about yourself are created through every experience you've had: the good, the bad, and the ugly.

Identify and weigh the self-limiting beliefs you currently hold by rating these statements on a scale from 0 to 4 based on how often you believe them; then add up the total score.

0 = Never, 1 = Rarely, 2 = Sometimes, 3 = Frequently, 4 = Always

I don't matter.

0   1   2   3   4

I'm not good enough.

0   1   2   3   4

I'm too old/young.

0   1   2   3   4

I don't deserve love/happiness.

0   1   2   3   4

I don't have enough time/experience.

0   1   2   3   4

I'll never find a better job, partner, etc.

0   1   2   3   4

Scoring:

16–24: You're carrying many self-limiting beliefs. Show yourself some compassion, and know that you're in the right place to address these beliefs.

6–15: You have room to grow. Keep working to make the improvements you deserve.

0–5: You're well on your way! Keep it up, and continue on your self-love journey.

From the Self-Limiting Beliefs Quiz, choose up to three limiting beliefs that are strongest for you. Where are they showing up in your life? Where do you think they came from? What is the evidence these beliefs are true or not true?

_____

_____

_____

_____

_____

_____

_____

_____

_____

_____

_____

_____

DO YOU KNOW YOUR VALUES?

Understanding your values is part of building confidence, a secure sense of identity, and a stronger relationship with yourself. This practice will help you identify your core values:

1. Gather ten pieces of paper.

2. Write "Who am I?" at the top of each piece.

3. Write one to two words to describe yourself on each one.

4. Write "Why?" three times down the left side of each piece of paper.

5. Write down an answer to each of the three whys for each paper.

6. When you're done, reflect on your responses to look for any patterns. Group together pages that seem similar to represent your core values.

> *Example:*
>
> Who am I? *A good communicator.*
>
> Why? *Because I believe good communication helps me feel understood.*
>
> Why? *Because I like to be open and honest with others.*
>
> Why? *Because being a good communicator is import ant to me.*

Who or what helped shape your core values, and how do you see them show up in your life? Are there places you could be truer to those values?

_____

_____

_____

_____

_____

_____

_____

_____

_____

_____

_____

_____

_____

YOU ARE WORTHY

Today's "hustle culture" tells us that worth comes from productivity. This couldn't be further from the truth. This exercise will help you redefine "worth."

Start by circling the answers that feel most accurate for you.

Productivity:

A. DEFINES MY WORTH.

B. IS MOST IMPORTANT.

C. IS THE ONLY THING THAT FULFILLS ME.

D. DOES NOT DEFINE ME.

Rest is:

A. LAZY.

B. NOT IMPORTANT.

C. MEANT TO BE EARNED.

D. NECESSARY.

Worth comes from:

A. WHAT I DO.

B. HOW MUCH I DO.

C. HOW WELL I DO WHAT I DO.

D. WHO I AM.

For questions to which you responded A, B, or C, write a new, positive definition for each word. It's okay if you don't fully believe the new definitions yet. Return to this exercise whenever you need a reminder.

YOUR NEW DEFINITIONS:

Productivity is _____.

Rest is _____.

Worth comes from _____.

Negative experiences, unhealthy relationships, and society's unrealistic expectations can teach you that worth is related to productivity, accomplishments, appearance, or financial status. What experiences have had a negative impact on your self-worth? How can you offer compassion to yourself around those experiences?

_____

_____

_____

_____

_____

_____

_____

_____

_____

_____

_____

_____

_____

_____

SOCIAL MEDIA CLEANSE

Social media comparisons can happen in many ways, and if you struggle with self-worth, comparison can contribute to feelings of self-doubt and not being enough. Instead of seeing a successful business owner online as inspiration, you may see them as another sign you're not doing enough to succeed. So, let's try a three-day social media cleanse: Choose three consecutive days to take a break from using your social media accounts.

At the end of your three-day cleanse, reflect on this experience in a journal. Write about whether you believe this break helped you stay true to your opinions and affected your self-worth, and whether you want to change your behavior on social media moving forward.

Your view of yourself plays an important role in what you do and the ways you interact with others. Make a list of ways you believe others view you, and write another list of ways you view yourself. Notice any differences. Where can you make improvements in how you view yourself?

_____

_____

_____

_____

_____

_____

_____

_____

_____

_____

_____

_____

SHATTER YOUR PERSONAL GLASS CEILING

"Glass ceiling" usually refers to the systemic barriers women and minorities face in the workplace, but I think you create your own glass ceilings, too, with the barriers you set for yourself through fears, self-limiting beliefs, and negative self-talk. The good news is that, with your own glass ceiling, you have more choices and power to overcome the barriers.

Write two self-limiting beliefs with a reframed supporting belief for each, and two negative self-talk statements with a reframed, accepting self-talk statement for each.

SELF-LIMITING BELIEF:

_____

_____

_____

SUPPORTING BELIEF:

_____

_____

_____

NEGATIVE SELF-TALK:

_____

_____

_____

ACCEPTING SELF-TALK:

_____

_____

_____

I am ready to let go of what no longer serves me and continue my journey of self-love.

BELIEVE IN YOURSELF

Have you ever felt like a fraud? Many women report experiencing imposter syndrome, which means they feel incompetent in some area of their life, even though they have experience and skills in that area. Try the following techniques to work on overcoming imposter syndrome:

1. Try using your name or "you" for affirmations and self-talk, rather than "I."

This creates the feeling that a more confident part of yourself is talking to the part that's doubtful. The confident part will help you remember relevant accomplishments and successes, which can relieve doubt.

Example: *Jordan, you have the training and experience you need to do this job well. You can do this.*

2. Talk about your feelings about imposter syndrome with someone you trust.

They may have experience with the same feelings, and even if they haven't, talking about it can release some of the weight of these feelings to help you manage them more easily.

NO MORE MASTER OF DISGUISE

As a child, were you ever teased for the way you dressed, how you sounded, or your taste in music? Early experiences such as these can teach us that different is wrong and you should blend in. But really, things that make you different also make you beautiful and interesting. The world would be boring (and honestly, a little creepy) if everyone was the same. Not owning your uniqueness can leave you feeling misunderstood, because it can be difficult to make meaningful connections when you're not living authentically. Instead, shift your perspective and celebrate your uniqueness.

When I was _____ , I was teased/judged because
                              age

I _____ .
          action/behavior/trait teased/judged for

This made me feel _____ . Now, I can see that
                         emotion

_____
          action/behavior/trait teased/judged for

made/makes me unique and there's nothing wrong with being

unique. Being unique actually makes me _____ .
                                        positive adjective

I'm proud to say I _____
                    action/behavior/trait teased/judged for

and I want to share that with _____ .
                              someone you trust

Think about a small mistake you made recently. Why did you make the choice or behave in the way that caused the mistake? What can you learn from that mistake, and how can you respond to that mistake now with self-compassion?

_____

_____

_____

_____

_____

_____

_____

_____

_____

_____

_____

_____

LET THEM FLOAT AWAY

During a third-grade snowball fight, I threw what I later learned was an ice ball that hit my classmate in the eye. And that classmate was my crush, of course! Although I've let go of this mistake, I share this to say that everyone messes up. Making mistakes is part of being human, and it's helpful to learn healthy ways to view and handle mistakes.

First, bring to mind up to five mistakes (that feel tolerable to contemplate) you would like to let go of. Then, write each on a separate cloud so the mistakes can gently float out of your mind.

On a scale from 1 to 10, how high is your expectation for yourself to not make mistakes or fail? Where did this expectation come from (e.g., parent's/caregiver's high standards)? How can you separate your self-worth from mistakes, failures, and perfectionism?

_____

_____

_____

_____

_____

_____

_____

_____

_____

_____

_____

_____

SET YOURSELF FREE

When you hold on to mistakes, you might ruminate on self-critical thoughts and carry painful emotions, such as guilt or shame. Forgiveness can help you break free and move forward. Choose one small mistake you've made and apply the Four As to practice self-forgiveness.

Write the Four As on a piece of paper with room to reflect on each. Try using this practice right after you make a mistake the first few times, until you start to feel comfortable with it. Once you're more comfortable, you can return to this practice if you start to ruminate on a mistake.

Acceptance. Accept responsibility for this mistake without judgment or criticism.

Awareness. Raise your own awareness of the emotions you feel around this mistake by writing about them.

Amendment. Apologize to or otherwise make amends with anyone affected by this mistake.

Absolution. Try not to ruminate on the mistake. Instead, focus on setting yourself free and moving forward.

Self-limiting beliefs and insecurities are often related to feelings of distrust (of yourself or others), not being enough, and not having enough. Name one self-limiting belief or insecurity you have that fits into each category. Imagine a future version of yourself who overcame these beliefs and insecurities. How did you achieve that?

_____

_____

_____

_____

_____

_____

_____

_____

_____

_____

_____

SELF-EMPATHY MEDITATION

This meditation will help you practice treating yourself with the same kindness you give to and receive from others:

1. Find a comfortable place to sit or lie down. Close your eyes and take a few deep breaths.

2. Visualize someone you love and who loves you.

3. Breathe in the love you receive from them and feel it flow throughout your body.

4. Replace your loved one with an image of yourself.

5. Imagine yourself going through a challenging time. Maybe when you made a mistake, were teased, or faced a difficulty.

6. As you let a breath out, imagine all the love you received from your loved one moving from your body to the image of you during that challenging time.

7. Visualize that love surrounding you.

8. Take a few deep breaths and gently open your eyes.

I always have been and always will be enough.

PROMPTS FOR BUILDING SELF-WORTH

SELF-WORTH IS AN INTERNAL SENSE that you are worthy and deserving of love, belonging, and care. Experiences of trauma or abuse, negative self-talk, and unrealistic societal expectations all can have a negative impact on your self-worth. Women in particular may be susceptible to unrealistic expectations around physical appearance or putting others' needs first. In this section, you'll build self-worth by developing skills to increase confidence, positive self-talk, trust in yourself, and admiration for your whole self: mind, body, and soul.

"We can cherish ourselves and our lives. We can nurture and love ourselves. We can accept our wonderful selves, with our faults, foibles, strengths, feelings, thoughts, and everything else. We are the best things we've got going for us. We are who we are and who we were meant to be. And we are not mistakes. We are the greatest things that will ever happen to us."

–MELODY BEATTIE

I'm a loving person, and that starts with believing I am worthy of love.

Describe what you believe a person with strong self-worth and confidence looks and acts like. What helps them feel so confident? How does their strong confidence and self-worth help them in their life and relationships?

_____

_____

_____

_____

_____

_____

_____

_____

_____

_____

_____

SELF-RELATIONSHIP ASSESSMENT

The relationship you have with yourself is your most important one. Without a healthy self-relationship, you are likely to have a harsh inner critic, not take care of your needs, and feel undeserving of happiness. Complete this assessment to see how you're doing with your relationship with yourself.

For each statement, circle the answer that applies to you.

1. I take care of my physical needs.

OFTEN / SOMETIMES / RARELY / NEVER

2. I use positive self-talk.

OFTEN / SOMETIMES / RARELY / NEVER

3. I know my wants and needs in life.

OFTEN / SOMETIMES / RARELY / NEVER

4. I'm aware of my emotions.

OFTEN / SOMETIMES / RARELY / NEVER

5. I regularly allow myself to do what I enjoy.

OFTEN / SOMETIMES / RARELY / NEVER

6. I feel confident in myself and my abilities.

OFTEN / SOMETIMES / RARELY / NEVER

7. I set healthy boundaries.

OFTEN / SOMETIMES / RARELY / NEVER

8 . I use assertive communication.

OFTEN / SOMETIMES / RARELY / NEVER

9 . I trust myself.

OFTEN / SOMETIMES / RARELY / NEVER

Reflecting on your responses, note your strengths as well as areas where you can improve your relationship with yourself.

_____

_____

_____

_____

_____

_____

_____

_____

_____

Some habits, such as self-care, help build healthy self-worth; others, such as negative self-talk or comparing yourself to other people, hurt it. What patterns do you see where you help or hurt your self-worth? Which harmful habit would you most like to improve?

_____

_____

_____

_____

_____

_____

_____

_____

_____

_____

_____

_____

ENJOY TIME WITH YOURSELF

Learning to enjoy time on your own is valuable because no matter how many people are in your life, you will always be alone at times. These times can teach you how you truly like to spend your time without the influence of others. Schedule whatever time works for you to do something enjoyable by yourself. You might try thirty minutes each day or one hour on a particular day each week.

Consider scheduling one of these activities, or come up with your own:

Read	Write	Take a walk	Meditate
Arts and crafts	Cook or bake	Pamper yourself	Take yourself on a date
Learn a new skill	Solo dance party	Watch a favorite movie	Listen to music or a podcast

Our brains have a negativity bias, which means we tend to focus on and be influenced by negative information and experiences more than by those that are positive. Remind yourself of your positives by listing at least ten of your strengths and accomplishments, no matter how small.

_____

_____

_____

_____

_____

_____

_____

_____

_____

_____

_____

_____

I'm a supportive and caring friend to my mind and body.

THE SELF-LOVE LANGUAGES

Gary Chapman identified The 5 Love Languages to help people understand how they and their loved ones prefer to give and receive love, and to help strengthen their relationships. For this exercise, transform the love languages into self-love languages to help strengthen your relationship with yourself.

First, read the descriptions of the self-love languages given in the chart. Then, on the opposite page, write in each heart one way to satisfy each self-love language for yourself.

PHYSICAL TOUCH	Focus on physical wellness and making your body feel good (e.g., gentle stretching)
ACTS OF SERVICE	Show yourself appreciation by doing things that make your life easier (e.g., organizing)
RECEIVING GIFTS	Gift yourself material or nonmaterial things (e.g., intentional time for rest)
QUALITY TIME	Give yourself undivided attention (e.g., reading without distractions)
WORDS OF AFFIRMATION	Use compassionate, encouraging words with yourself (e.g., affirmations)

PHYSICAL
TOUCH

ACTS OF
SERVICE

WORDS OF
AFFIRMATION

RECEIVING
GIFTS

QUALITY
TIME

Humor is a great tool to help yourself break free from the negativity bias by making situations feel lighter. When you laugh, endorphins release in your brain and have a positive impact on your confidence and mood. List eight things that make you laugh (e.g., movies, videos, pictures). Come back to this list whenever you need stress relief and a positive shift.

_____

_____

_____

_____

_____

_____

_____

_____

_____

_____

CHANNEL YOUR INNER TIGER

My husband and I recently bought artwork of a house cat looking in the mirror and painting himself as a tiger. Not only is the picture adorable, but it also has a lovely meaning. Wouldn't it be great if we could all see and believe in the power within us?

Take a cue from the house cat and draw, paint, or sculpt yourself in a positive, confident light. What does your inner confidence look like: a queen, a superhero, maybe a lioness? Have fun and tap into your confidence and creativity.

PRACTICING HOW TO SAY NO

When you struggle with self-worth, you might look to other people for approval and feel like others' needs are more important than yours. Saying no can be a challenge when you have a fear of disappointing or not being liked by others. Try thinking ahead about situations where you might want to say no to something, and plan what you'll say.

To compete this exercise, read through the examples of situations where you might want to say no. Practice writing a response to each situation, and notice how your emotions are affected. Then, on the following page, come up with real-life examples of situations where you want to say no and fill in the blank fields of the table.

REQUEST	IF YOU SAY YES, YOU'LL FEEL	HOW YOU'LL SAY NO	WHEN YOU SAY NO, YOU'LL FEEL
Boss asks you to take on another project	Overwhelmed	I can't take on anything else right now.	Relieved
Friend invites you to a party this weekend	Tired	Thank you for thinking of me, but I can't make it. Hopefully I can next time!	Content

REQUEST	IF YOU SAY YES, YOU'LL FEEL	HOW YOU'LL SAY NO	WHEN YOU SAY NO, YOU'LL FEEL
Family member asks you to split the cost of a gift that is more than you can afford.			
Doctor tries scheduling appointment at a time you could go but strongly prefer not to.			

How would your past self be proud of who you are today? What can you start doing now to help ensure you'll be proud of yourself in five years (e.g., setting healthier boundaries, choosing healthier relationships)?

_____

_____

_____

_____

_____

_____

_____

_____

_____

_____

_____

_____

KNOWING WHEN TO SAY NO

When you place so much value on the approval of others, saying yes can become an automatic response, which can make it difficult to understand when to say no. Take the time to think about and listen to your emotions before saying yes or no. Try the following:

- **When someone asks something of you, say, "Let me get back to you," or something similar.**

- **Check in with your emotions right then, or later, when you have the time.**

  - Sit in a quiet, comfortable place for at least three minutes.

  - Focus on your breathing and what emotions come up.

    Example: If you feel anxious about saying yes, this can be a sign to say no.

- **If you're still unclear, reflect on these questions:**

  - If I say yes, would this:

    ○ Violate any of my boundaries?

    ○ Misalign with my wants, needs, and values?

    ○ Be coming from a place of fear or guilt?

    Example: A yes answer to any of these questions could indicate that a no response may be best.

SEVEN SIGNS YOU'LL BENEFIT FROM MORE SELF-TRUST

Self-trust is interconnected with self-worth and self-love, because it involves staying true to yourself, being kind to yourself regardless of the outcome of your decisions, and believing in your abilities. Self-doubt, negative self-talk, and experiences such as trauma can contribute to losing trust in yourself.

Circle the number by each statement that shows up in your life, and fill in the blanks with an example:

1. I second-guess myself and my decisions (even very small ones).

_____

_____

2. I seek external validation and ask for others' opinions frequently.

_____

_____

3. I'm easily persuaded to change my opinions or values.

_____

_____

4. I don't try new things or take risks.

_____

_____

5. I do things to prove my value to others.

_____

_____

6. I self-sabotage or break promises to myself.

_____

_____

7. I don't listen to my instincts.

_____

_____

People tend to trust those who are consistent, show care, and communicate well. How can you apply these qualities to build self-trust by showing up for yourself consistently and offering yourself compassion and positive self-talk?

_____

_____

_____

_____

_____

_____

_____

_____

_____

_____

_____

_____

GETTING UNSTUCK

All-or-nothing thinking involves making negative generalizations that can keep you feeling stuck in self-doubt and unhelpful habits. These inflexible thoughts are common symptoms of self-doubt and perfectionism; they say things are all good or all bad with no in between.

On the left, list four negative generalizations you hold about yourself. Then try using the "and" approach to get unstuck and practice flexible thinking for each one.

Example:

I always make mistakes.　　　*I made a mistake and I can do it differently next time.*

_____　　_____ *and*

　　　　　　　　　　　　　　_____

_____　　_____ *and*

　　　　　　　　　　　　　　_____

_____　　_____ *and*

　　　　　　　　　　　　　　_____

_____　　_____ *and*

　　　　　　　　　　　　　　_____

A negative or critical view of your physical appearance can also affect your self-worth. Describe the body stereotypes held in your culture, family, the media, etc., and how they have influenced you. How can you challenge them?

_____

_____

_____

_____

_____

_____

_____

_____

_____

_____

_____

_____

CONFIDENT YOGA

Physically moving helps build confidence by improving the way your body feels and the way you feel about your body. The Warrior 2 yoga pose takes up more physical space than some other poses—a good parallel to taking up space in your life in other ways, such as speaking up for yourself. If this pose is physically unavailable to you, hold any comfortable pose that takes up space.

1. Stand with feet spread about 3 to 4 feet apart.

2. Turn your left foot out 90 degrees.

3. Bring your hands to your hips and relax your shoulders.

4. Extend your arms straight out to your sides with your palms down.

5. Bend your left knee until your knee is over your ankle (only go as far as is comfortable).

6. Turn your head to look out over your left hand.

7. Hold for five deep breaths. Repeat on the right side.

List six things you are grateful for about your physical characteristics and body type, and note why you are grateful for each.

_____

_____

_____

_____

_____

_____

_____

_____

_____

_____

_____

_____

_____

TAKE A MINDFUL GRATITUDE WALK

Spending time outside enhances self-worth because it reduces stress and can bring a different perspective to your life and yourself. Practice mindful body movement outdoors to help you appreciate your body and take the focus off its appearance. You can also do this practice seated if that's more comfortable for you.

As you walk, pay attention to how your:

- **Lungs help you breathe**

- **Nose helps you smell**

- **Arms and legs move you forward with each step you take**

- **Feet feel on the ground**

- **Skin allows you to feel the fresh air**

- **Brain helps you function**

After your walk, reflect on how you feel physically and emotionally.

PROMPTS FOR HEALING YOUR RELATIONSHIPS

HUMANS ARE SOCIAL BEINGS, which means the ways you think and feel about yourself affect how you connect with and relate to others. Many women are raised to socialize in ways that do not put themselves first, resulting in unhealthy relationship patterns, such as codependency and people pleasing, and ultimately, resentment and burnout. Part of self-love is surrounding yourself with healthier relationships, with people who make you feel safe, valued, and respected. Working through this section will help you clarify what you want from relationships, as well as help you practice other important relational tools, such as establishing healthy boundaries, dealing with toxic people and behaviors, and being assertive.

"Now I understand that in order to feel a true sense of belonging, I need to bring the real me to the table and that I can only do that if I'm practicing self-love."

– BRENÉ BROWN

For others, being in your life is a privilege, and the people you choose to surround yourself with can have an impact on your self-worth. Consider the important relationships in your life. Who are those people, and how do they make you feel about yourself?

_____

_____

_____

_____

_____

_____

_____

_____

_____

_____

_____

_____

WHAT ARE YOUR NEEDS?

Understanding what you need allows you to communicate your needs more confidently and get those needs met, which can help you feel more fulfilled in your relationships. Answer the following questions with one important relationship in mind.

For the first question in each pair, circle how important the need is for you. For the second, circle the degree to which that need is being met in the relationship you're focusing on.

1. **I want to feel safe physically, mentally, and emotionally.**

STRONGLY AGREE / AGREE / DISAGREE / STRONGLY DISAGREE

2. **I feel safe physically, mentally, and emotionally.**

STRONGLY AGREE / AGREE / DISAGREE / STRONGLY DISAGREE

1. **I want to feel valued and for someone to take interest in what I'm doing.**

STRONGLY AGREE / AGREE / DISAGREE / STRONGLY DISAGREE

2. **I feel valued and interesting.**

STRONGLY AGREE / AGREE / DISAGREE / STRONGLY DISAGREE

1. I want to feel appreciated and respected.

STRONGLY AGREE / AGREE / DISAGREE / STRONGLY DISAGREE

2. I feel appreciated and respected.

STRONGLY AGREE / AGREE / DISAGREE / STRONGLY DISAGREE

1. I want to feel encouraged and supported.

STRONGLY AGREE / AGREE / DISAGREE / STRONGLY DISAGREE

2. I feel encouraged and supported.

STRONGLY AGREE / AGREE / DISAGREE / STRONGLY DISAGREE

Reflecting on your responses in the What Are Your Needs? questionnaire, which needs are most important to you? Where are the discrepancies between your important needs and the way they are being met? For any important needs that aren't being met yet, how can you communicate them?

_____

_____

_____

_____

_____

_____

_____

_____

_____

_____

_____

_____

BOUNDARIES FOR YOUR JOURNEY

Healthy boundaries are essential to self-love. They aim to protect your time and energy, increase self-worth, and improve relationships. Consider how different types of boundaries fit into your self-love journey.

TYPES OF BOUNDARIES	WHAT TO RESPECT
Emotional	Feelings and emotional capacity
Mental	Ideas and beliefs
Physical	Personal space and physical touch
Material	Limits around money and possessions
Time	Use of time

1. On a piece of paper, write a self-love goal related to your use of time.

2. List one to three boundaries you need to set for yourself to make that goal possible. Apply them over the next few weeks.

EXAMPLE:

Goal: I want to have thirty minutes to myself each day.

Boundaries: I will not accept any meetings during my lunch break. Also, I will close my door and turn off my phone during my break.

3. Once you've applied the boundaries related to your time goal, continue this practice to create a goal for each type.

How did the people with whom you grew up communicate or respect boundaries? How are they practiced now within your family and friend groups?

_____

_____

_____

_____

_____

_____

_____

_____

_____

_____

_____

_____

Asking for what I need does not mean I'm needy.

POROUS, RIGID, OR HEALTHY

In Nedra Glover Tawwab's book *Set Boundaries, Find Peace*, she explains the differences between porous, rigid, and healthy boundaries. Your boundaries may differ depending on the relationship or environment. You might have healthy boundaries at work and porous boundaries at home, or rigid boundaries with a parent and porous boundaries with a friend.

Notice which relationships come up for you as you read the following descriptions. Place them where they fit in the table on the following page.

POROUS	HEALTHY	RIGID
Oversharing	Sharing appropriately with others	Never sharing
Difficulty saying no		Building walls
People pleasing	Not depending on others' opinions	Avoiding vulnerability
Codependency	Feeling comfortable saying no	Enforcing strict rules
Accepting mistreatment	Standing firm in your values	High expectations for others

POROUS	HEALTHY	RIGID

Where do you need healthier boundaries in your life? What tells you that you need them (e.g., feeling resentful toward someone)? Write down some answers below, and then practice talking about the healthy boundaries you need out loud.

_____

_____

_____

_____

_____

_____

_____

_____

_____

_____

_____

_____

DEALING WITH GUILT

Feelings of guilt about setting boundaries often come from the other person's response, *anticipation* of the other person's response, or feeling uncomfortable with putting your needs first.

Follow these tips to become the best boundary-setter you can be:

- **Sit with the guilt.** Feeling guilty doesn't mean the boundary you're setting is wrong.

- **Use self-compassion.** Acknowledge the guilt you're feeling without judgment.

- **Avoid taking responsibility for others' reactions.** You're responsible for communicating your boundary respectfully but not for another person's reaction to it.

- **Adjust your mindset.** Setting boundaries isn't selfish or disrespectful. Boundaries improve relationships with others.

- **Set more boundaries.** You'll likely feel less guilty about setting boundaries the more you practice.

Fear of a negative reaction (e.g., guilt-tripping, defensiveness) is a common barrier to setting boundaries. Consider one boundary you'd like to set and the reasons you fear a negative reaction will follow. Create a plan for how to deal with that reaction.

_____

_____

_____

_____

_____

_____

_____

_____

_____

_____

_____

_____

CHANGING THE AVOIDANCE CYCLE

When you avoid negative thoughts and emotions by overscheduling yourself, not trusting or speaking up for yourself, or taking care of others' needs at the expense of your own, it can take a toll on your self-worth and, by extension, your relationships. The following diagrams are based on Melanie Fennell's cognitive behavioral model (1997), and can help you become aware of how your thoughts, emotions, and behaviors interact to influence your self-worth.

The example below shows how negative beliefs can feed a cycle of low self-worth. Fill in the cycle on the next page with a positive belief to see how that changes the emotions and behaviors.

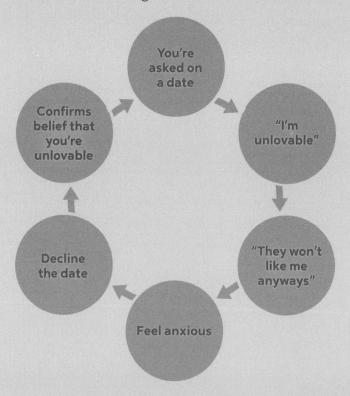

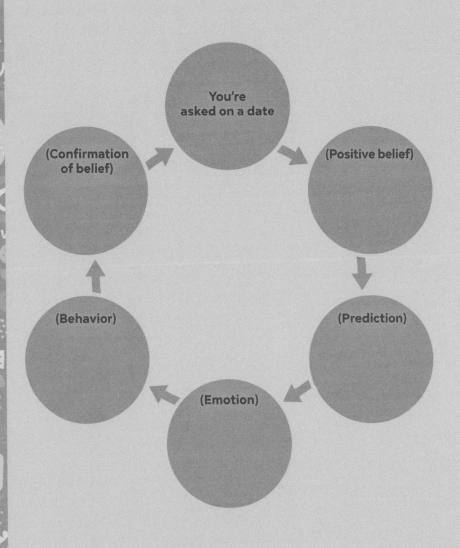

LET'S BE REALISTIC

When you hold unrealistic expectations, you're likely to feel disappointed, frustrated, and resentful of others when they can't meet those expectations. Three ways you may hold unrealistic expectations are:

- **Expecting yourself from other people**

  Example: Expecting your partner to do the dishes the same way you do them

- **Expectations based on "shoulds"**

  Example: Believing people should like you because you put their needs first

- **Not communicating expectations**

  Example: Not being clear about your expectations, or believing others should already know what you expect from them

Practice identifying your expectations and communicating them:

1. On paper, write down an expectation you hold for an important relationship in your life that you think may be unrealistic.

2. Reflect on how you can adjust it to be more fair, compassionate, and loving.

3. Have an open discussion with your partner, parent, friend, etc., about this expectation.

WHAT IS A HEALTHY RELATIONSHIP, REALLY?

Knowing what a healthy relationship is seems like it would be obvious, but without a good model, it can be difficult to recognize the qualities of a healthy relationship.

Circle the qualities you believe describe a healthy relationship:

Honesty	Name-calling	Mutual respect
Individuality	Manipulation	Shared values
Intimidation	Open communication	Mutual give and take
Support	Compromise	Limited privacy
Only spend time together	Accusations	
Fair fighting	Have fun together	

As you build self-worth, you gain the ability to see yourself, others, and the world differently. How can building your self-worth improve your ability to deal with other people's unhealthy behaviors, such as lying, being jealous, name-calling, or acting controlling?

_____

_____

_____

_____

_____

_____

_____

_____

_____

_____

_____

_____

_____

BE ASSERTIVE, B-E ASSERTIVE

Assertive communication is about clearly stating what you think, feel, need, or want in a respectful, direct, and nondefensive way. The skills of assertive communication include both verbal and nonverbal behaviors.

Check the assertive behaviors that you'd like to work on.

☐ Stop apologizing unnecessarily.

☐ Identify your wants and needs, and ask for them to be met.

☐ Believe your feelings, wants, and needs are just as important as those of others.

☐ Express negative thoughts and feelings in healthy ways.

☐ Know your limits and say no when necessary.

☐ Accept compliments and feedback well.

Practice writing an assertive response to this scenario:

> **You notice your partner hasn't been contributing to the chores at home for the past week.**

_____

_____

_____

Knowing your relationship attachment styles can improve how you understand yourself and your relationships. Complete the attachment style quiz at Web-Research-Design.net/cgi-bin/crq /crq.pl. After you take the quiz, reflect on your results here.

_____

_____

_____

_____

_____

_____

_____

_____

_____

_____

_____

_____

CONFRONTING CONFLICT ROLE-PLAY

Conflict is uncomfortable, isn't it? It's also inevitable in any long-term relationship. It often seems like avoiding it is the easier option, but working through conflict in healthy ways is an important part of building and maintaining close relationships. If you avoid conflict, your relationships may feel less fulfilling and leave you sacrificing your own needs.

Practice facing conflict and responding assertively to help build your tolerance for the discomfort that arises. Choose someone you feel comfortable with to role-play the suggested scenarios, or create your own:

- **A coworker consistently interrupts you during meetings.**

- **A family member engages in an argument with you.**

- **You disagree with the way your partner disciplined your child/pet.**

If you've been on a plane, you've heard the flight attendant announce that you need to put your own oxygen mask on before you can help anyone else. Where do you need to put yourself first in your everyday life? How will your life look different when you start putting yourself first in these ways?

_____

_____

_____

_____

_____

_____

_____

_____

_____

_____

_____

_____

_____

ALWAYS THE HELPER, NEVER THE HELPED

With low self-worth, codependency, or people pleasing, you might find your value in being the helper. On paper, there's nothing wrong with that. It becomes harmful, though, when you place your whole value on helping or don't see your value outside of being in the helper role. Neglecting yourself in favor of helping others can lead to frustration, burnout, and even physical illness. It can also lead you to being taken advantage of. As you start to ask others for help and to see your value outside of helping, you may find yourself moving toward relationships where there is a healthier balance of give and take. It's time for you to practice asking for the help you're used to giving.

Choose one small task you can ask for help with or delegate this week.

EXAMPLES:

- **Ask your partner for help with the dishes.**
- **Use a delivery service for groceries.**

I have to take care of myself before I can care for anyone else.

PROMPTS FOR EMBRACING WHO YOU ARE

YOUR COMMITMENT TO building self-love is admirable. In this section, you'll bring together everything you've learned and explore ways to apply your new knowledge moving forward. You'll keep working on becoming your own best friend and expressing gratitude for the journey you're on. As you focus on your goals and dreams, you'll find ways to ease further outside your comfort zone and stay motivated to continue on this beautiful journey of loving and accepting all parts of yourself, while also allowing the best version of yourself to shine through.

"When you have made good friends with yourself, your situation will be more friendly, too."

– PEMA CHÖDRÖN

Reflect on what stood out to you in each section of this journal. What were your biggest takeaways? Write at least one for each section.

_____

_____

_____

_____

_____

_____

_____

_____

_____

_____

_____

_____

AUTHENTICALLY YOU QUIZ

As you learn to love yourself, you start to acknowledge and eventually accept parts of yourself that were buried or ignored. You may be reencountering these parts or meeting them for the first time. This quiz will give insight into where you are in regard to embracing your whole self and living authentically.

Rate each statement on a scale of 1 to 4.

0 = Never, 1 = Rarely, 2 = Sometimes, 3 = Often, 4 = Very Often

I allow myself to be silly.

0   1   2   3   4

I do the things I enjoy, no matter what anyone thinks.

0   1   2   3   4

I live by my values.

0   1   2   3   4

I embrace my weirdness and quirks.

0   1   2   3   4

I love the parts of me that are unique.

0   1   2   3   4

I know what makes me happy, and I do it.

0   1   2   3   4

For the statements you responded to with a 3 or 4, congratulations on the progress you've made! Keep on growing and learning. For the statements you responded to with a 1 or 2, what's holding you back from embracing them more often? Which would you most like to work on?

_____

_____

_____

_____

_____

_____

_____

_____

_____

_____

_____

YOUR AFFIRMATION MEDITATION

This journal provides two affirmations for you in each section (for example, on page 115). Affirmations can be even more powerful when they come from your voice and address what's most meaningful to you.

List three affirmations that speak to you. Then, as you complete the meditation below, repeat these affirmations on each inhale, as noted by the phrases in italics.

1. Close your eyes and bring your attention to your breath.

2. Take three deep breaths, inhaling through your nose and exhaling through your mouth.

3. As you inhale, welcome *your first affirmation* into your mind. Exhale slowly.

4. On the next inhale, welcome *your second affirmation.* Exhale slowly.

5. Repeat for *your third affirmation.*

6. Take deep breaths for another minute or as long as you feel comfortable.

Part of embracing where you are is acknowledging how far you've come. Celebrate yourself! List four things you can reward yourself with at the end of each week for the next month as you continue living with self-love (e.g., buy a new shirt, take a long walk). Add them to your schedule.

REFER YOURSELF

Write a letter as if you were referring yourself to be friends with someone else, by acknowledging how amazing you are at being a friend to yourself. If you're not there yet, think about the ways you are a good friend to others and how you want to treat yourself when you become your own best friend.

I believe _____ is the best candidate to be your
              your name

friend because they are _____ , _____ ,
                              three positive adjectives

and _____. We have so much fun _____
                                         solo activity you enjoy

together. When I'm feeling down, they encourage and support

me by _____ . I could go on
              compassionate words or actions

all day about how great they are, and they're working hard to

see how _____ and _____ they are, too.
              two positive adjectives

_____ will be an amazing friend to you.
     your name

Gratitude helps increase your ability to navigate pain and allows you to see more of the good in yourself and the world around you. Set a timer for five minutes and write everything you're grateful for about your self-love journey.

_____

_____

_____

_____

_____

_____

_____

_____

_____

_____

_____

ACCEPTING MYSELF AS I AM

Cooking is not my thing, and after a few years of feeling badly about it, I've accepted that I do simple foods best (we're talking Greek yogurt and baked sweet potatoes simple). I feel so much better since accepting this, and I hope you can continue bringing acceptance to your whole self, too.

On a piece of paper, list three things you're having trouble accepting about yourself; write an accepting self-talk statement next to each one. This list can serve as a reminder that you're human and that it's both normal and okay to have imperfections.

> **Example:** *I'm not good at cooking. → I enjoy that simple meals still nourish me while allowing more time in my schedule.*

Bring in some humor with a cartoon of one thing on your list. You might use a picture you find online or in a magazine, or draw your own. I drew a picture of myself burning dinner with a big smile on my face.

Sometimes, with change and growth come loss and grief. Some things may no longer serve you as you grow in your self-love. What relationships and coping skills might you release as you take this journey? How would you like to honor this grief?

_____

_____

_____

_____

_____

_____

_____

_____

_____

_____

_____

_____

_____

_____

SELF-LOVE BINGO

Let's play a game. Try to complete one row of bingo this week (five in a row across, down, or diagonally) and then continue on to finish the whole board. Feel free to adapt with your own ideas.

Said no	Identified an item of gratitude	Spent time alone	Reflected on my values and needs	Showed appreciation for my body
Practiced saying an affirmation	Checked in on progress toward my goals	Did something fun	Listened to my Joy Playlist	Slept for seven to eight hours
Spent leisurely time outside	Practiced a meditation	Completed this journal!	Spoke kindly to myself	Watched TV/read a book without checking my phone
Drank eight or more glasses of water	Took a break from social media	Set a boundary with someone	Engaged in a hobby	Named something I love about myself
Spent time with a loved one	Reframed negative self-talk	Tried something new	Allowed myself to take a break	Practiced a self-soothing activity

CALLING DR. SELF-LOVE

Remember asking for a permission slip to go to the nurse's office in school? Now you get to give yourself permission to practice and engage in the aspects of self-love that are most important to you or that you struggle with the most.

Get ten sticky notes, and write yourself a permission slip on each one. Place these notes in places you see often, such as a bathroom mirror or car dashboard. Use the following examples or create all ten by yourself. Feel free to be creative.

- I give myself permission to be kind to myself.

- I give myself permission to set the boundaries I need.

- I give myself permission to forgive myself for past mistakes.

TRACK YOUR GROWTH

Studies show it takes around two months to form a new habit. Research also shows that missing the habit occasionally doesn't significantly hinder the habit-forming process, which is helpful information for challenging those all-or-nothing thoughts.

Track your growth on one self-love habit for the next two months (e.g., doing yoga, practicing self-kindness). The flowers shown represent eight weeks. Use one flower each week; color in one leaf a day for the first six days and the flower for the seventh day you complete the habit. At the end of each week, reflect on your progress.

You can come back to this journal many times throughout your journey of self-love. Name two areas that you feel are the most important for you to focus on the next time you return to it. Why did you choose these areas?

_____

_____

_____

_____

_____

_____

_____

_____

_____

_____

_____

TAKE IT ONE STEP AT A TIME

Sometimes people hold unfair expectations for themselves, believing they'll go straight from self-criticism to self-love, but there are other steps along the way. Although this journey isn't linear, and you might stay on a particular step for a while or go back to a previous step, understanding it in this way can help you figure out the next step to work toward if you find yourself stuck in self-criticism or even self-neutrality and want to be in a place of self-love.

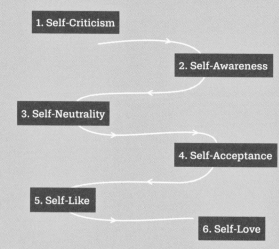

EXAMPLE:

1. I hate the way I look.

2. I'm aware that I don't like how my face looks.

3. I have a round face.

4. This is how my face looks.

5. I like how my face looks.

6. I love myself no matter how I look.

Now, fill in the blanks with your own examples of what your self-talk might sound like at each step.

1. Self-Criticism: _____

_____

2. Self-Awareness: _____

_____

3. Self-Neutrality: _____

_____

4. Self-Acceptance: _____

_____

5. Self-Like: _____

_____

6. Self-Love: _____

_____

Use the references at the back of this journal (page 148) and at Audible.com/blog/article-best-self-love-podcasts to create a list of books and podcasts you want to explore to continue growing in self-love. Write your list here.

_____

_____

_____

_____

_____

_____

_____

_____

_____

_____

_____

_____

I accept myself unconditionally for who I have been, who I am now, and who I will be.

TRY SOMETHING NEW

You may already have stepped out of your comfort zone while completing this journal. Continue that growth by stepping out of your comfort zone in other ways. This helps you grow, engage with your curiosity and creativity, and have fun. Start small and gradually build your confidence.

Choose one of these ideas to try this week or select your own:

- Go for a walk in a new area.
- Try a new recipe for dinner.
- Listen to a new musical artist.

Regular check-ins and reflecting on your goals and dreams are important to embracing where you are and acknowledging where you want to go. Choose one small self-love goal to focus on this week, and create a step-by-step plan to reach it (e.g., set one boundary).

_____

_____

_____

_____

_____

_____

_____

_____

_____

_____

_____

_____

SELF-COMPASSION CAN KEEP YOU GOING

The self-love journey can be challenging, and at times you may feel stuck or discouraged about continuing. When you feel this way, instead of motivating with self-criticism, which is based in shame and fear, try motivating with self-compassion, which is based in love and kindness. Do this as either a writing or a meditation exercise.

1. **Find a quiet space** to focus on your breathing, and then widen your focus to the following questions or write responses to the questions on paper.

2. **Identify what's getting in the way.** What negative self-talk or limiting beliefs are making you feel stuck or discouraged on your self-love journey?

3. **Encourage yourself.** What do you need to hear to make a change? What would a nurturing friend, parent, or teacher tell you to help you move forward?

4. **Reframe self-talk.** Talk to yourself with love and encouragement to continue moving forward. Remind yourself that you deserve to grow in self-love.

I choose to fill
the rest of my life
with self-love.

A FINAL NOTE

You've self-reflected, faced difficult situations, practiced self-compassion and self-forgiveness, released self-limiting beliefs and self-doubt, learned tools to help you build confidence and self-worth, and explored how to create healthier relationships with yourself and others. I hope you're proud of yourself. I know I'm proud of you for all the hard work you've put into building your self-love.

Although it's a lifelong journey, every step you take along the way is important and worth celebrating. From saying no one more time to catching one more negative self-talk thought, remember to acknowledge and appreciate all the small steps you take that move you toward loving yourself. On the following pages, you'll find some bonus journaling pages so that you can continue to record your thoughts and feelings as you continue your self-love journey.

Thank you for allowing me to be a part of your journey. I'm grateful to have had the opportunity to share with you the self-love activities and concepts that helped me and many of my clients on their journeys. I'll leave you with a final reminder: You deserve all the love and kindness you want and need, and that includes the love you can give yourself.

SELF-LOVE
REFLECTIONS

_____

_____

_____

_____

_____

_____

_____

_____

_____

_____

_____

_____

_____

REFERENCES

"Alternate Activity 1: Empathy Meditation." Unitarian Universalist Association. Accessed March 12, 2023. uua.org/re/tapestry /youth/call/workshop4/171803.shtml.

Between Sessions Interactive. "Becoming More Assertive." 2015, PDF download.

Borysenko, Joan. "Module 1: How to Help Clients Heal from Deeply Internalized Judgment." In Ruth Buczynski's online course *Working with Core Beliefs of "Never Good Enough."* National Institute for the Clinical Application of Behavioral Medicine. nicabm.com/confirm/never-good-enough.

Beattie, Melody. *Codependent No More.* New York: Spiegel & Grau, 2022.

Brown, Brené. *The Gifts of Imperfection.* Hazelden Information Educational Services, 2010.

Chapman, Gary. *The 5 Love Languages: The Secret to Love That Lasts.* Chicago: Northfield Publishing, 2015.

Chödrön, Pema. *When Things Fall Apart.* Boulder, CO: Shambhala, 2000.

"Cognitive Behavioral Model of Low Self-Esteem (Fennell, 1997)." *PsychologyTools.* Accessed 1 April, 2023. psychologytools .com/resource/cognitive-behavioral-model-of-low-self-esteem -fennell-1997.

Doyle, Glennon. *Untamed.* New York: The Dial Press, 2020.

Earley, Jay, and Bonnie Weiss. "The Seven Types of Inner Critics." *IFS Growth Programs.* Accessed March 11, 2023. personal -growth-programs.com/the-seven-types-of-inner-critics.

Earnshaw, Elizabeth. *I Want This to Work.* Louisville, CO: Sounds True, 2021.

Elle, Alexandra. *After the Rain.* San Francisco: Chronicle Books, 2020.

Falk, Megan. "The Essential Yoga Poses for Beginners, According to an Instructor." *Shape.* Accessed March 18, 2023. shape.com /fitness/workouts/yoga-poses-for-beginners.

Gardner, Benjamin, Phillippa Lally, and Jane Wardle. "Making Health Habitual: The Psychology of 'Habit-Formation' and General Practice." *British Journal of General Practice* 62, no. 605 (December 2012): 664–666. DOI: 10.3399/bjgp12X659466.

Germer, Christopher, and Kristin Neff. *Teaching the Mindful Self-Compassion Program.* New York: The Guilford Press, 2019.

Glover Tawwab, Nedra. *Set Boundaries, Find Peace.* New York: TarcherPerigee, 2021.

Levine, Amir, and Rachel Heller. *Attached: The New Science of Adult Attachment and How It Can Help You Find And Keep Love.* New York: TarcherPerigee, 2010.

Neff, Kristin. "xercise 7: Identifying What We Really Want." *Self-Compassion.* Accessed March 26, 2023. self-compassion .org/exercise-7-identifying-really-want.

Neff, Kristin. *Self-Compassion.* New York: HarperCollins, 2011.

Picture of *Self-Love Does Not Happen Overnight*, 2020, The Positive Way 8.

Picture of *The Self-Love Languages.* 2017, Self-Love Rainbow.

Walker, Jason R. "One Powerful Tool to Clarify Who You Really Are." *Medium*, February 15, 2020. medium.com/the-ascent/one -powerful-tool-to-clarify-who-you-really-are-9b10a94b0344.

ACKNOWLEDGMENTS

As a therapist, I can say there are no better teachers than my clients. I am thankful to all my clients, past and present, who have helped me continue to grow to become the person and therapist I am today.

Thank you to my husband, my grandpa, and everyone else who has loved and supported me along the way as I've learned how to love myself.

ABOUT THE AUTHOR

 Jordan Brown, LPC, has served a wide variety of populations and, within the past three years, has focused her work on helping young women navigate anxiety and self-worth. She opened her Wisconsin-based private practice in 2020 and expanded to a group practice in 2022. She is passionate about helping her clients gain more awareness and acceptance, and the ability to see their potential and how wonderful they are. Outside the office, Jordan enjoys spending time with her husband and their two cats, Diggle and Pepper; being active; and traveling, especially anywhere with an island vibe, an ocean, and a beach.